SCREAMING

SOUL

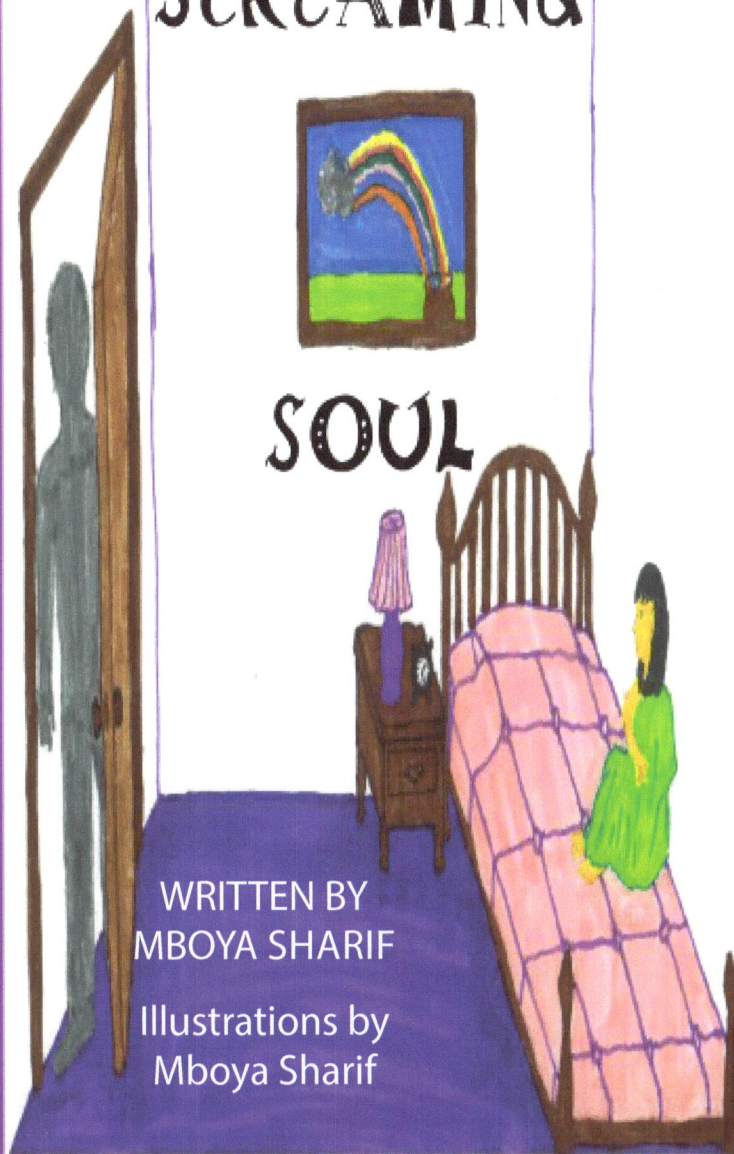

WRITTEN BY
MBOYA SHARIF

Illustrations by
Mboya Sharif

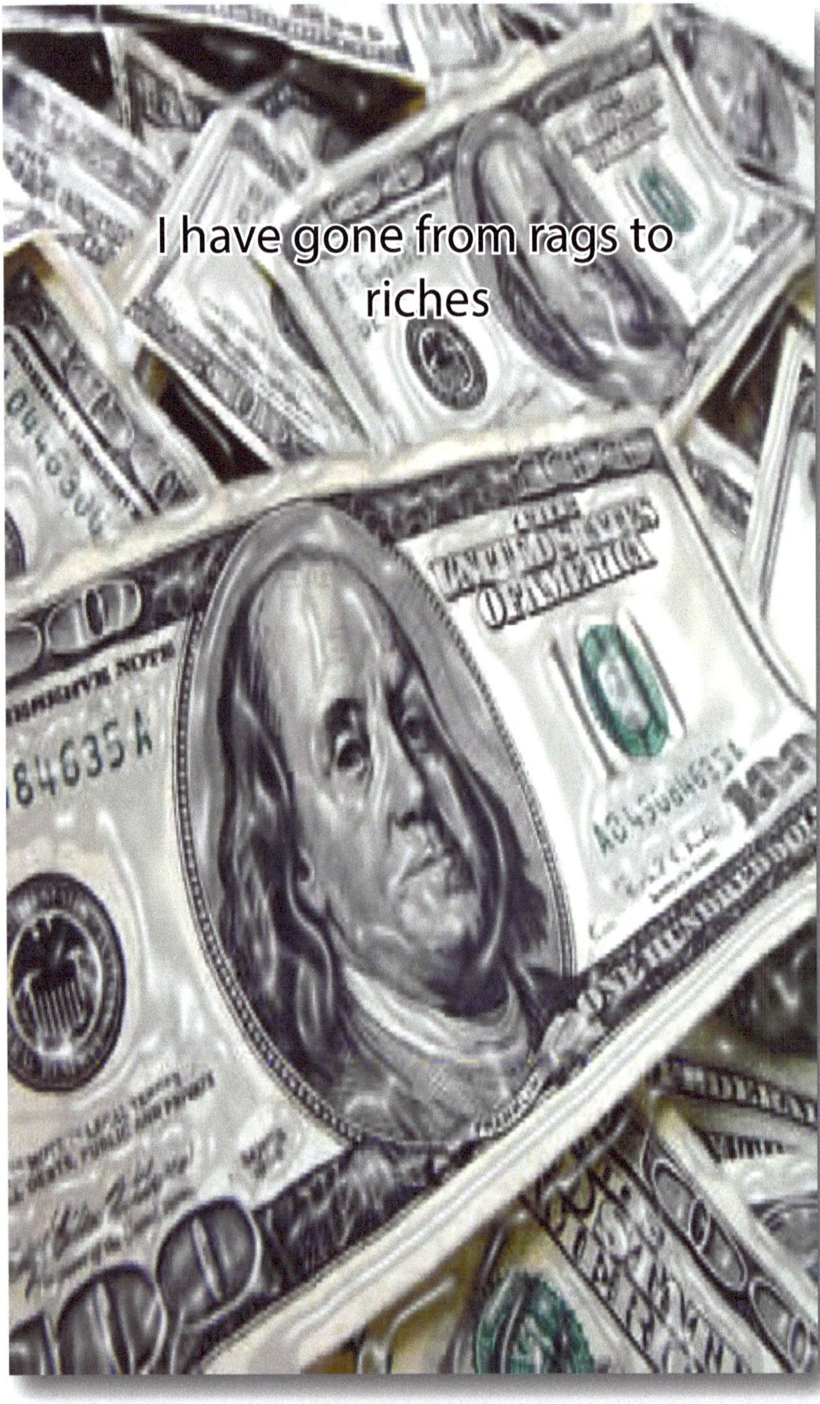
I have gone from rags to riches

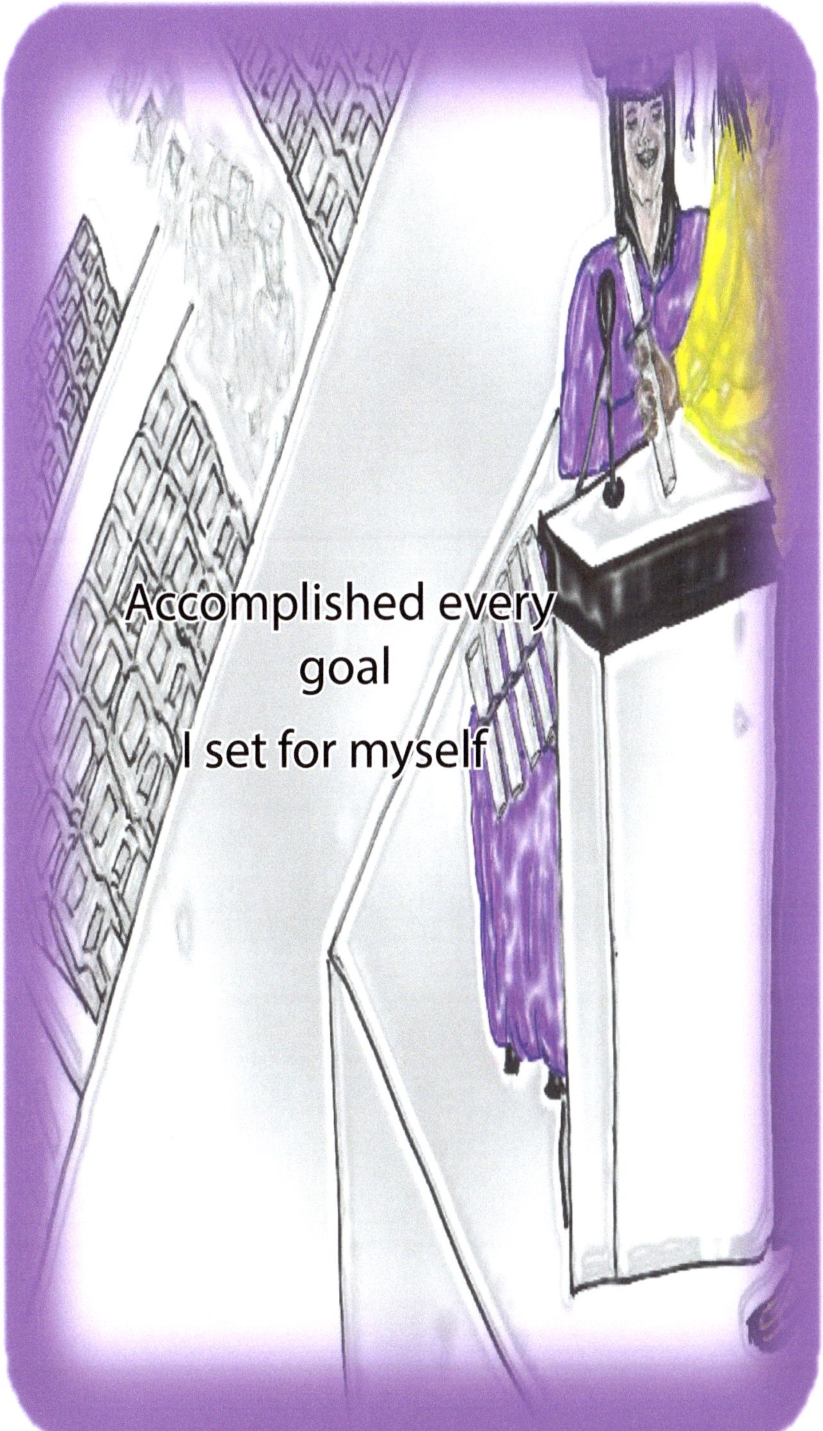
Accomplished every goal
I set for myself

I have
achieved
much wealth

Look at me!

I am the person

You want to be

But don't be fooled by my
outer shell

Because my soul inside
Is screaming in hell

No matter how much I
Try to douse the fire

My soul is screaming

"HIGHER AND HIGHER!"

I try so hard to
Hide the pain

In doing so
It has my mind
Going insane

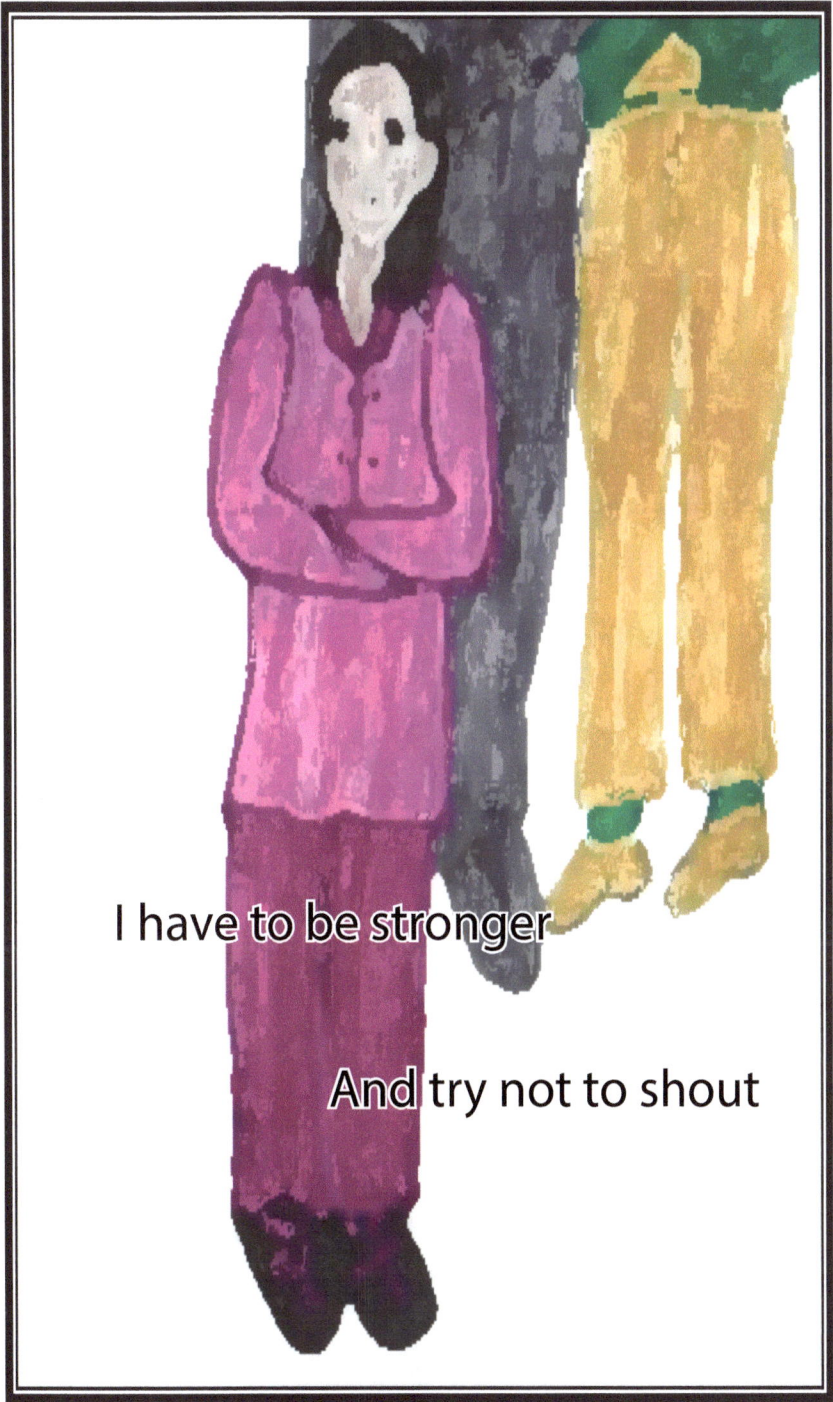

I have to be stronger

And try not to shout

"I

WANT TO TAKE
MYSELF OUT!

FOR WHAT YOU HAVE
DONE!"

But I have to think about
My kinfolk and believe there's hope

But my soul has been crying ever since I've been nine

You told me it was okay
I believe every word you say

And didn't tell anyone
About that day

And will that get

my soul out of hell?

Every day I see your face
When I bow my head and say my grace
You're across from me
Thanking God!
For the food you're about to receive

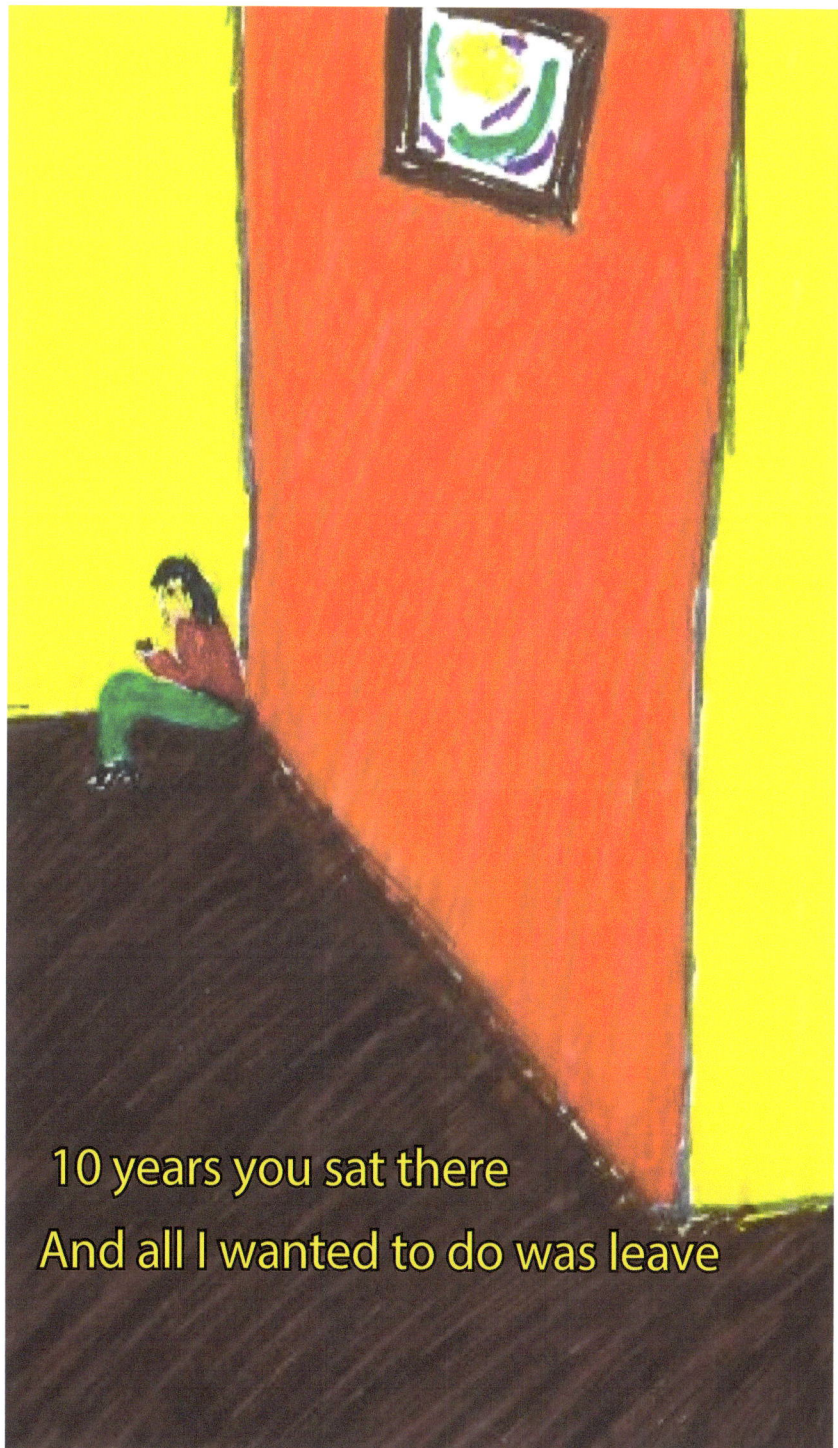

10 years you sat there
And all I wanted to do was leave

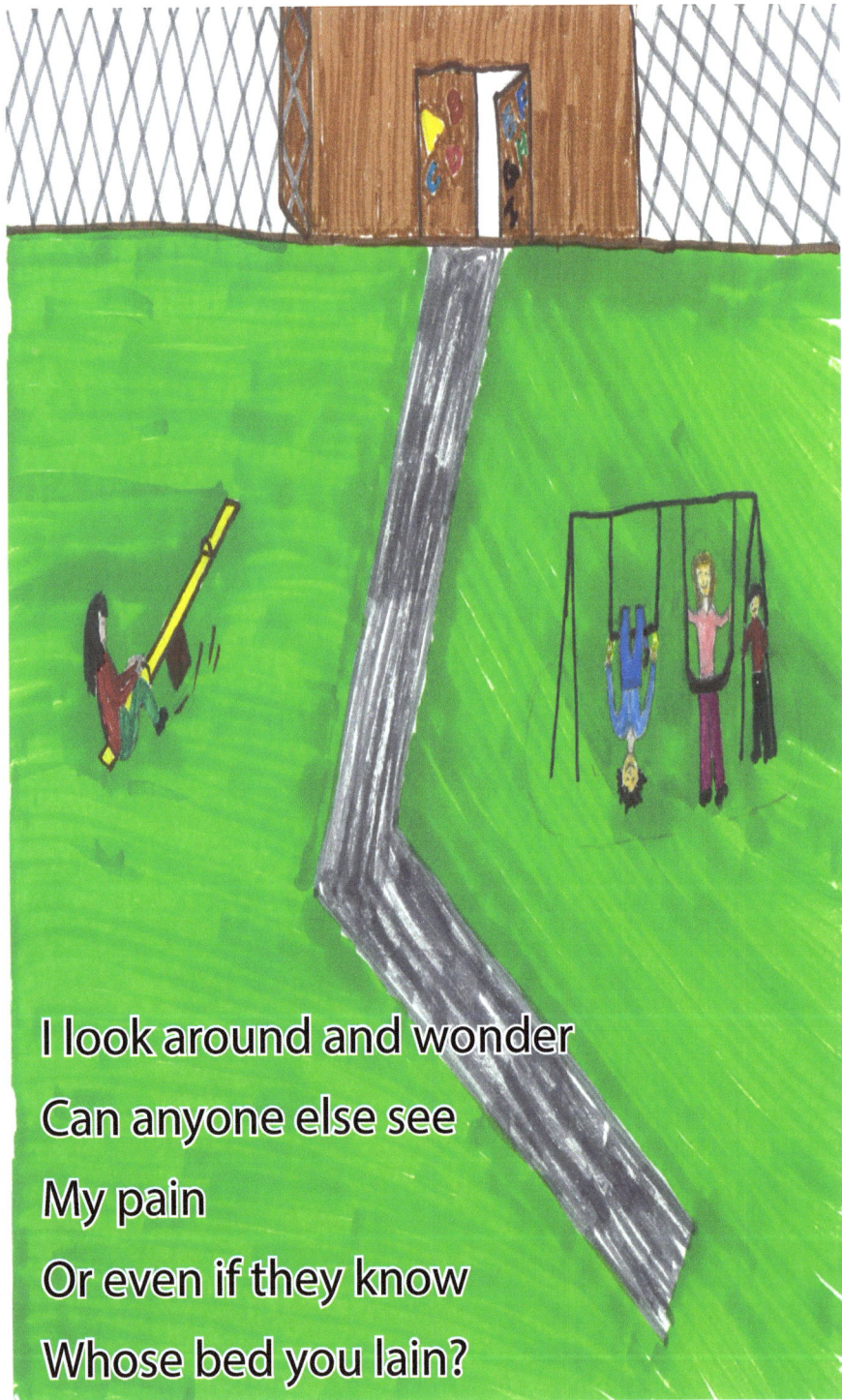

I look around and wonder
Can anyone else see
My pain
Or even if they know
Whose bed you lain?

"I

SAID I WANT TO TAKE MYSELF OUT!"

FOR WHAT YOU PUT ME THROUGH!"

"NO!"

Maybe I'll just kill YOU!

But I know my heart won't let

YOU

Get the best of ME

So I will just holster

My emotions

And let God deal with you
Before I do something
I won't regret!

When an unwanted situation comes into our lives, there is always someone we want to tell but we are afraid to. Write a letter to 2 people you would like to tell about your situation. No one will read it but you unless you choose to share. Be honest! Here are letters from different screaming souls who agreed to allow me to share their story. These are their heartfelt stories unedited. At the end of these letters there will be room for you to compose your heartfelt story.

8/27/93

Dear "Father",

I am writing to explain to you why I chose not to attend your baby daughters christening. Congratulations on your marriage and child, I am glad you have finally figured out what you want to do with your life. I only regret that you did not do it much, much sooner. About 17 years sooner, before I met you when you were playing the role of Catholic Priest. When I met you I was a sophomore in high school, just 15 years old, but already very troubled and vulnerable. When you befriended me I was truly honored, out of all the other boys and girls you made me feel very special. I was very comfortable talking to you about my problems and at that time in my life I needed a friend to help me sort through all of the adolescent confusion. I was feeling pretty much alone and afraid in this world, and I was totally alienated from my parents as many teenagers are at that age. You represented someone whom I respected, admired and could trust, a spiritual counselor and confident.

Then you betrayed that trust in the most horrendous way possible. You violated and abused my body, my mind and my soul because of your uncontrolled lust. In a position of authority, you took advantage of me in a sick, disgusting self-centered way. In plain old English, a warped 50 year old Catholic Priest sexually molested a vulnerable 15 year old repeatedly for years. I was 18 before I could refuse your advances but the damage was already done. I'm sure I wasn't the only one. I'll bet you had lots of little friends like me.

I believe it was your premeditated intent to get me drunk by filling me full of scotch and then raping me before I even knew what hit me. At the time I did not have the skills to know how to stop this nightmarish victimization from happening. All I knew how to do was blame myself and internalize the guilt and shame I felt, growing sicker as the years went by. I was so devastated when I woke up after realizing what had happened, that I felt that I had committed the worst possible sin there ever could be.

I felt like I had slept with Jesus Christ himself, and I was the lowliest person on earth. Since I did not know how to extricate myself from this situation it happened again and again and again. I then became alienated from any type of religion or spirituality as I saw myself as unworthy of God's love or forgiveness. For the next 10 years I continued to search for peace in the form of any type of alcohol or drugs I could find. Anything to drown out the pain I was feeling. I do not blame you for my addiction, but I do blame you for the lack of spirituality in my life until I found recovery at the age of 25. You destroyed any belief or faith in anyone or anything spiritual that I did have prior to meeting you. Since finding recovery from addiction some 7 years ago it has continued to be a struggle to regain any faith in religion, much less in men. Through recovery and 2 years of costly additional therapy I have grown to the point of trusting again and I have the strongest faith I have ever had. I have a wonderful husband and we are expecting our first child. I will never forgive you for the harm and pain you have caused in my life, and I no longer have to pretend that you're that wonderful priest that everyone thought helped me so much. That is why you were not invited to my wedding or my baby's christening in the future. I wouldn't want you anywhere near my baby girl (or boy). Please stay far away from me and my family, including my parents. I have not told them of this yet but I'm not sure I never will. At this time I do not plan to initiate legal action against you, giving you back the pain and suffering I have kept silent about may be enough. Oh, and one other thing for you to think about as you look at your newborn daughter: there are many more people like you out there, just waiting to take advantage of a vulnerable little girl. Watch over her and pray for her, that she never has to endure what you

Dear Stepfather,

I just need to ask you one question, one question that may take away the hurt and ease the pain. Why?? Why did you hurt me? Why did you take my childhood away from me? Why? You stole from a child and I was stupid enough to trust you. You lied to me and told me everything was going to be alright. Well it wasn't alright! Well it wasn't alright. My heart aches and my heart is in pain with fear of when is the next time you my stepfather will climb on top of me you now 10 year old step daughter.

The first time it happened when I was 7 years old I didn't know was going on. You told me to be quit e and be a good girl. Well a good girl is not what I am now 14 years old acting out for attention not sure if my mom loves me or even care. You made me feel hopeless, ugly and scared and that wasn't enough for you. You made me go out and look for love because that's what I thought if was all about. I had no clue.i had no idea that the boys I met that smile at me and said I wa cute. I had no idea that I shouldn't be having sex. I didn't know you could love someone without giving yourself up to them. I just didn't know. You should have taught me the right way to love and to be love but you were to busy loving me the wrong way instead of being a guide for me and or an example you made me the example of what stepfathers shouldn't do to their daughters. How could you…..who gave you permission to get in my bed with me.

Many times people are afraid or unable to express their real emotions to themselves or others. The next exercises may help you vocalize them.

Exercise 1

ILLUSTRATION A

Emotions are part of our lives. In order to live we all have to feel. What

feelings do you want to come across? Find the different emotions.

A	D	D	I	T	I	A	A	A	P	E	S	Y	Z	C
L	B	E	B	H	A	A	N	N	O	C	A	S	K	R
P	A	R	F	G	C	N	G	X	G	B	A	U	W	F
O	P	T	Y	A	C	H	I	U	Z	E	R	O	Q	H
R	V	A	C	S	U	P	O	E	M	X	R	L	X	I
A	J	H	P	O	S	S	A	O	R	R	O	A	Z	R
E	R	L	O	O	I	A	F	K	L	J	G	E	J	R
F	A	A	D	L	N	K	S	V	N	P	A	J	J	O
X	H	C	T	W	I	P	A	S	H	S	N	J	L	M
N	Y	I	O	P	G	Z	X	B	Y	S	C	E	P	A

1. OFFENSIVE
2. ROMANTIC
3. LOVE
4. FEAR
5. SADNESS
6. HATRED
7. ACCUSING
8. ANGER
9. ARROGANCE
10. JEALOUSY

Word definitions

	Life	Achieve	Justice
	Obstacles	Proximity	Disguise
	Shape	Clout	Fit in
	Hatred	Triumph	Clemency
	Power	Conceive	Relief
	Expected	Integrity	Regurgitate
	Repeat	Help	Barriers
	Inexorable	Forgiveness	Existence
	Create	Conform	Silhouette
	Cover up	Antipathy	Closeness

Study the words above. Find the words that have the same meaning.

Example: The definition of conform is fit in. Put words and definition on the lines below.

Conform/Fit in _____   _____

_____   _____

_____   _____

_____   _____

_____   _____

_____   _____

                            _____

Dear

Dear_____

Dear_____

Dear_____

Dear_____

_____

_____

_____

_____

_____

_____

_____

_____

_____

_____

_____

_____

Dear_____

Dear_____

_____

_____

_____

_____

_____

_____

_____

_____

_____

_____

_____

_____

_____

Dear_____

Dear_____

Dear_____

_____

_____

_____

_____

_____

_____

_____

_____

_____

_____

_____

_____

Dear_____

Dear_____

Dear_____

_____

_____

_____

_____

_____

_____

_____

_____

_____

_____

_____

_____

_____

Dear_____

Dear

Dear_____

_____

_____

_____

_____

_____

_____

_____

_____

_____

_____

_____

_____

Please Note:

Screaming Soul is not meant to be a substitute for professional care and services. You should always consult a trained professional with any questions about your specific needs and concerns.

SCREAMING SOUL:

There are many times in life that we fear we are alone.
What happened to you is not your fault! No One
deserves the cruelty you went/going through.

Excerpts from others stories:

Dear Stepfather,

"You stole from a child and I was stupid enough to
trust you. You lied to me and told me everything
was going to be alright. Well it wasn't alright! My
heart aches and my heart is in pain with fear..."

Dear "Father"

"For the next 10 years I continued to search for peace
in the form of any type of alcohol or drugs I could
find. Anything to drown out the pain I was feeling. I
do not blame you for my addiction, but I do blame
you for the lack of spirituality in my life until I found
recovery at the age of 25. You destroyed any belief
or faith in anyone or anything spiritual that I did
have prior to meeting you. Since finding recovery
from addiction some 7 years ago it has continued
to be a struggle to regain any faith in religion, much
less in men."

www.ingramcontent.com/pod-product-compliance
Lightning Source LLC
Chambersburg PA
CBHW041524090426
42737CB00038B/116